A New True Book

GLOBES

By Paul P. Sipiera

CHILDRENS PRESS®

CHICAGO

The Strait of Gibraltar and the
Mediterranean Sea as viewed from
a satellite orbiting the Earth

PHOTO CREDITS
The Bettmann Archive—7, 9, 17 (left), 22 (left), 29

NASA—4

North Wind Picture Archives—8 (left), 13 (top), 15, 17 (top right)

Photri—38

Courtesy of Replogle Globes, Inc.—44

© P. P. Sipiera—8 (right), 11, 25, 41 (left), 45 (left); Spaceslides, 45 (right)

SuperStock International, Inc.—6, 19, 37, 40; © NASA, 2; © David Spindell, 20; © Kitagawa II, 24; © William G. Pearce, 41 (right)

TSW-CLICK/Chicago—© Tony Craddock, 12

UPI/Bettmann Newsphotos—Cover, 18

Official U.S. Navy Photo—43

Valan—© Kennon Cooke, 13 (bottom)

Yerkes Observatory—35 (3 photos); © Richard Dreiser, 17 (bottom right)

Art by Charles Hills—22 (right), 26, 27, 30, 31, 33

Cover—Replogle Globe Company

To the memory of my uncle, Tony Blazejack.

Library of Congress Cataloging-in-Publication Data

Sipiera, Paul P.
    Globes / by Paul P. Sipiera
        p.   cm. — (A New true book)
    Includes index.
    Summary: Describes the usefulness of globes to
show the roundness of the Earth and various
consequences of that shape.
    ISBN 0-516-01124-3
    1. Globes—Juvenile literature. [1. Globes.]
I. Title.
GA260.S57   1991   91-15869
912—dc20   CIP
                                       AC

TABLE OF CONTENTS

The Earth as seen by the Apollo 17 astronauts
heading toward the Moon

WHAT IS A GLOBE?

What does the Earth look like? How far is the United States from England? Where is Antarctica? You can find the answers to questions like these on a globe.

A globe is really a model of the Earth. It is round. It has oceans, mountains, and countries marked on it.

A simple globe can show countries, ocean currents, and shipping routes.

A globe is different from a map. Globes are round and maps are flat. Maps do not show the true shape of the Earth. It is very hard to draw a flat map of a round Earth.

6

WHAT DOES
THE EARTH LOOK LIKE?

A long time ago,
everyone thought the Earth
was flat. They thought the
sky was a half circle above
the Earth. They thought
the Earth was the center of

An ancient
illustration of
what the
universe might
look like

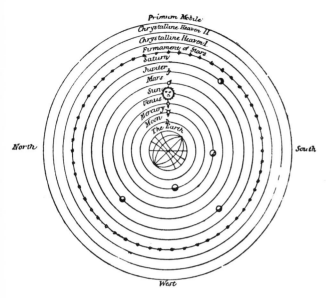

Ptolemy, the ancient astronomer, pictured the Earth
as the center of the universe (left). The circular shape
of the Sun is easily seen at sunset (right).

the universe, and everything
moved around it.

The Sun, the Moon, and
the stars seemed to move
across the sky. People
believed in what their eyes
saw. But they were wrong!

ANCIENT ASTRONOMERS USED THE CIRCLE

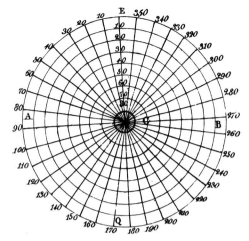

An early drawing
of a circle
divided into
degrees

No one knows who
discovered the circle,
but it was to answer
many questions about
the universe.

Ancient mathematicians
divided the circle into 360
parts. We now call these
parts degrees. Astronomers
used the circle to represent

the sky. They also used it to measure the positions of heavenly bodies like the Sun and the planets.

The Sun, the Moon, and the stars all appear to move across the sky with a circular motion. People observed this motion for hundreds of years. They learned how to predict where these objects would be day after day.

Astronomers, living north of the equator, observed that the Sun rose directly in the east on the first day

Ancient people used Stonehenge as a calendar for predicting seasons.

of spring. As it moved
west, it was directly south
when it reached its
highest point. As it set in
the west, it had traveled
through a half circle.

Knowing about the rising
and setting positions of

The horizon is the point where the sky appears to meet the land.

the Sun was very important to farmers. They learned to use the changing position of the Sun to mark seasons. This helped them know when to plant their crops and when to harvest them.

PROOF OF A ROUND EARTH

In the fourth century B.C., the Greek philosopher Aristotle came to believe that the Earth was round like a circle. He learned this by observing an eclipse of the Moon. An eclipse happens when the Moon passes into the Earth's shadow. And the

Aristotle (above) studied the Moon (below). He observed that the Moon moves from right to left and passes into the round shadow of the Earth.

Earth's shadow was round!
Only round objects cast
round shadows. Therefore, the
Earth had to be round, too.

Aristotle listened to the
stories told by sailors.
They spoke of how familiar
stars disappeared as strange
new stars appeared above
the horizon. They said this
only happened when they
sailed from north to south.
To Aristotle, this was proof
that the ships were sailing
over a curved surface.

Eratosthenes, a Greek

An ancient astronomer
measuring the angle
of a star above
the horizon

living in the third century
B.C., also believed the
Earth was round. He used
what he knew about the
circle to measure the size
of the Earth. To do this, he
measured the angles of
shadows.

He knew that on the first day of summer, a stick in the ground at the city of Syene, Egypt, cast no shadow. At the same moment, a similar stick placed in the ground at Alexandria, Egypt, did cast a shadow. By using geometry, Eratosthenes was able to determine the angle formed between the two cities and the Earth's center. He then had the distance between Syene and Alexandria measured.

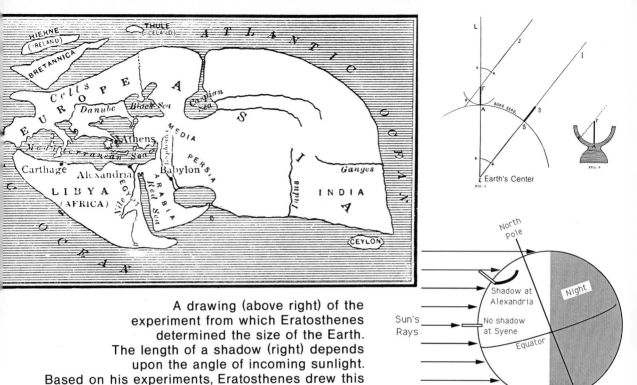

A drawing (above right) of the experiment from which Eratosthenes determined the size of the Earth. The length of a shadow (right) depends upon the angle of incoming sunlight. Based on his experiments, Eratosthenes drew this map of the world in the third century B.C.

Eratosthenes used these measurements to figure out the circumference of the Earth. He multiplied the distance between the cities by the number of times the angle is contained in 360 degrees.

17

Earthrise, as seen from lunar orbit, shows a definitely round planet.

Through the use of simple observations and measurements, geometry proved the Earth was round. And now its size was known, too.

WHY IS A GLOBE USEFUL?

A globe can do much more than just show the shape of the Earth. Many globes have the boundaries of the world's countries marked on them.

Modern globes provide much more information than just the shape of the Earth.

Relief globes show the high and low places of the Earth's surface.

Some globes have raised areas to show mountains. These are called relief globes.

The colors used on a globe also can tell you things. Oceans and lakes are blue. Deserts may be shown in yellow or brown.

LATITUDE AND LONGITUDE

Modern globes are crossed by lines called latitude and longitude. The use of latitude and longitude goes as far back as the time of Claudius Ptolemy. He lived in Egypt in the second century A.D.

Ptolemy used lines of latitude and longitude to locate places on the Earth's surface.

These lines are not straight lines. They are

Claudius Ptolemy was the greatest geographer of his time.

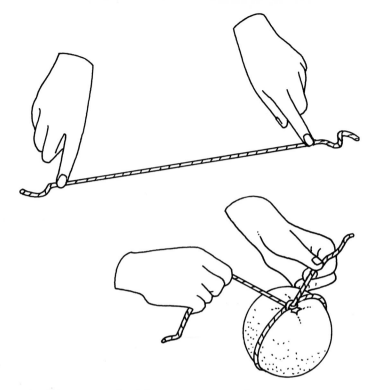

A string stretched between two points makes a straight line. The same string stretched across a round object makes a circle.

circles or parts of circles that go around the Earth. The Earth is round, and it is not possible to draw a straight line on a curved surface.

USING LATITUDE AND LONGITUDE

Almost every place on the Earth has a latitude and longitude reference. Only the North and South Poles use just latitude. This is because all lines of longitude come together at the poles.

The equator is a line of latitude. It divides the Earth into two equal parts—the Northern Hemisphere and the Southern Hemisphere.

All lines of longitude join at the North and the South Poles.

All the lines of latitude
run parallel to the equator.
They measure distance
north or south of the equator
in degrees. The equator has
a latitude of zero degrees.
The North Pole and the
South Pole have a latitude
of 90 degrees.

The lines of longitude
run from the North Pole to
the South Pole. They are
called meridians. One of
these is very important. It
is called the prime meridian.

The prime meridian
passes through Greenwich,

The prime meridian
is clearly marked
at the Royal
Observatory in
Greenwich, England.

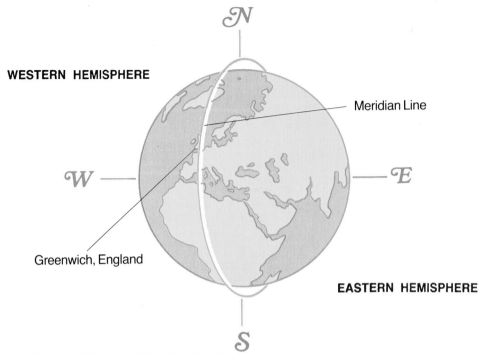

WESTERN HEMISPHERE

Meridian Line

Greenwich, England

EASTERN HEMISPHERE

The prime meridian divides the Earth
into Eastern and Western hemispheres.

England. It is used to
divide the Earth into the
Eastern Hemisphere and
the Western Hemisphere.
Meridians west of Greenwich
have a western longitude.
Meridians east of Greenwich
have an eastern longitude.

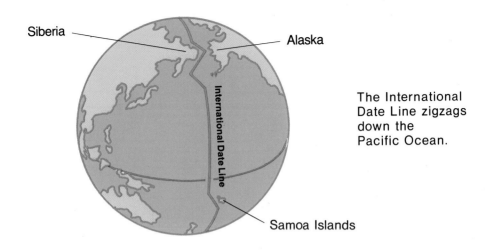

Siberia Alaska

International Date Line

Samoa Islands

The International Date Line zigzags down the Pacific Ocean.

Halfway around the world from the prime meridian is an imaginary line called the International Date Line. On a globe it is not a straight line. Instead, it zigzags down the Pacific Ocean.

It was agreed long ago that the International Date Line would not cross the

27

boundaries of countries. It
must remain over international
waters to avoid problems.

Each day on the Earth
begins at the International
Date Line. West of this
line, it is early morning on
Monday, while east of the
line it is still late night on
Sunday.

Lines of longitude are
also used to mark time
zones. The equator is
divided into 24 units of 15
degrees each. The Sun
appears to travel through

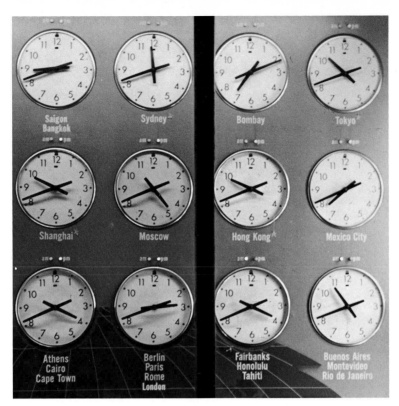

Different cities have different times because of their geographical locations.

one of these units each hour. Each unit represents a different time zone. When it is 8 P.M. in London, it is 2 P.M. in Chicago.

Time zones are based on the position of the Sun

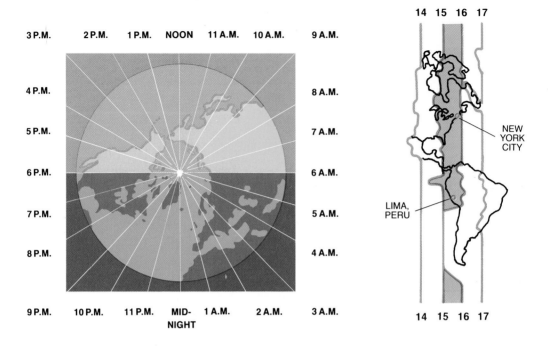

3 P.M.	2 P.M.	1 P.M.	NOON	11 A.M.	10 A.M.	9 A.M.

4 P.M.   8 A.M.

5 P.M.   7 A.M.

6 P.M.   6 A.M.

7 P.M.   5 A.M.

8 P.M.   4 A.M.

9 P.M.	10 P.M.	11 P.M.	MID-NIGHT	1 A.M.	2 A.M.	3 A.M.

14 15 16 17

NEW YORK CITY

LIMA, PERU

14 15 16 17

Above: Half the Earth is in daylight, while the other half is in darkness. Every 15 degrees of a circle equals one time zone.

relative to the Earth's surface. New York City and Lima, Peru, share the same time even though Lima is far south of New York City. This is because they are within the same 15-degree unit of longitude. The same is not true for

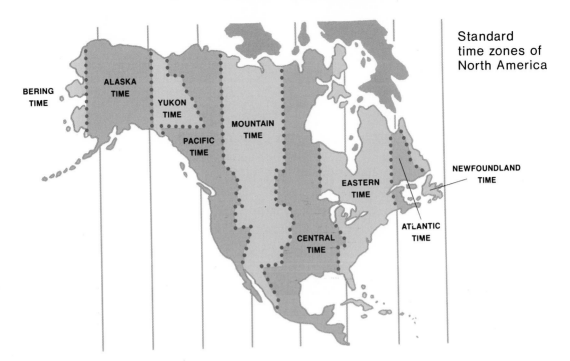

latitude. New York City
and San Francisco have
nearly the same latitude.
But when it is 4 P.M. in
New York City, it is only
1 P.M. in San Francisco.
This is because they are
separated by three time
zones, or about 45

degrees of longitude. The Sun is not in the same position for each location.

Special lines of latitude are used to mark seasonal change. They mark the position of the Sun as it appears to move north or south of the equator each year.

The Sun stands directly overhead at noon on the equator twice each year. These two days mark the beginning of the spring and fall seasons.

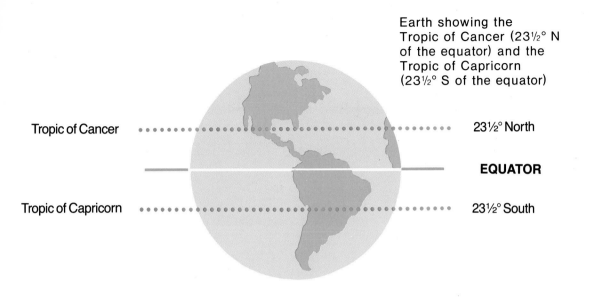

Earth showing the
Tropic of Cancer (23½° N
of the equator) and the
Tropic of Capricorn
(23½° S of the equator)

Tropic of Cancer   23½° North

EQUATOR

Tropic of Capricorn   23½° South

Those places where the Sun stands directly overhead only once a year are called the Tropic of Cancer and the Tropic of Capricorn. The Tropic of Cancer is the circle of latitude that is 23½ degrees north of the equator. The

33

Tropic of Capricorn is 23½ degrees south of the equator.

When the Sun reaches the Tropic of Cancer, it is summer for people living in the Northern Hemisphere. Winter begins in the Northern Hemisphere when the Sun reaches the Tropic of Capricorn.

The seasons are reversed in the different hemispheres. In the Northern Hemisphere, summer occurs during June, July, and August. In

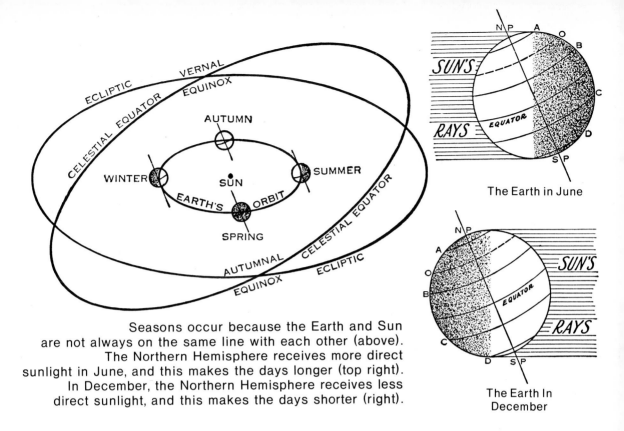

ECLIPTIC

CELESTIAL EQUATOR

VERNAL EQUINOX

AUTUMN

WINTER

SUN

EARTH'S ORBIT

SUMMER

SPRING

CELESTIAL EQUATOR

AUTUMNAL EQUINOX

ECLIPTIC

The Earth in June

SUN'S

RAYS

EQUATOR

The Earth In December

SUN'S

RAYS

EQUATOR

Seasons occur because the Earth and Sun
are not always on the same line with each other (above).
The Northern Hemisphere receives more direct
sunlight in June, and this makes the days longer (top right).
In December, the Northern Hemisphere receives less
direct sunlight, and this makes the days shorter (right).

the Southern Hemisphere,
summer occurs during
December, January, and
February.

This happens because
the Earth is tilted on its
axis by 23½ degrees, so
the northern half of the

35

Earth receives more direct sunlight in June than in December. The more direct the Sun's rays, the warmer the weather will be. In December, the Sun's rays come in at a low angle, and the weather is much colder.

There are two other important circles of latitude. They are the Arctic Circle in the north and the Antarctic Circle in the south. Each is 66½ degrees from the equator.

People enjoy the Midnight Sun in Norway.

Above the Arctic Circle, the
Sun shines from March 21st
to September 21st. This area
is called the Land of the
Midnight Sun because the
Sun never sets for these
six months.

Sunrise as seen from Earth Orbit. For people living in the shadow area, it is still night.

Then, from September 22nd to March 20th, the Sun never rises. For six months, it is dark. Because of the tilt of the Earth on its axis, the direct rays of sunlight miss the polar regions.

In the Antarctic region, the six-month periods of day and night are reversed.

FINDING PLACES ON THE EARTH

Every city and town on Earth has its latitude and longitude reference. This makes it much easier for airline pilots to find their destinations because it pinpoints exact locations.

Finding your exact location is not always easy. Early navigators measured the height of the Sun at noon to determine their latitude position. At night they measured the

Once sailors depended on the positions of the Sun and stars to find their location on the Earth.

height of the North Star, if they were in the Northern Hemisphere. When they knew the height of the Sun or the North Star above the horizon, they could use angles to locate their position on the Earth.

Longitude was much

Official time on the Earth is kept at the Royal Observatory in Greenwich, England (left). Modern navigation instruments (right).

more difficult to determine. It was not until the invention of accurate clocks that longitude could be determined. The time at the prime meridian, which runs through Greenwich, England, would serve as the standard for all ship's navigators.

Ships would carry a clock that was set to Greenwich time. This clock showed the time at 0 degrees longitude. To determine the ship's longitude position, the time at the ship's location was measured by the position of the Sun at noon. When the two times were compared, the navigator could tell the ship's distance from Greenwich in degrees of

longitude.

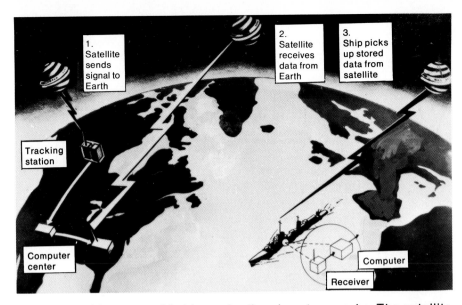

An example of how a worldwide navigational system works. The satellite signal (left) is picked up by a receiving station, which sends it to another center to interpret and transmit data back to the satellite that is now over a different part of the Earth. Ships with receiver-computer equipment use the position of the satellite with earlier satellite signals (phase 1) to determine the ship's position on the Earth.

Today modern navigators use radio beacons from orbiting satellites to help them find their location on the Earth. Yet, all positions are still reported in terms of latitude and longitude.

OUT-OF-THIS-WORLD GLOBES

Some globes represent objects other than the Earth. A celestial globe shows all the star constellations.

This celestial globe locates 1,200 stars as they appear within their constellations.

The Moon globe (left) shows the positions of craters, mountains, and maria (seas). This Mars globe (right) was made from photos taken by the Mariner 9 spacecraft in 1971.

Today, globes are made to represent the Moon and some planets, such as Mars. Someday we may have globes for all the planets. For now, we can study a globe to learn about our own planet Earth.

45

WORDS YOU SHOULD KNOW

angle (ANG • gil) — the shape made by two lines that meet at a point

Antarctic Circle (ant • ARK • tik SER • kil) — an imaginary circle around the Earth, located at 66½ degrees south of the equator

Arctic Circle (ARK • tik SER • kil) — an imaginary circle around the Earth, located at 66½ degrees north of the equator

astronomer (ast • RAH • nih • mer) — a person who studies stars, planets, and other heavenly bodies

axis (AX • iss) — an imaginary straight line that runs through the Earth from north to south and around which the Earth turns

boundaries (BOUND • reez) — imaginary lines that mark edges, such as the boundaries of a country

celestial (sih • LESST • chil) — of the sky and the planets, stars, etc.

circumference (ser • KUM • frince) — the distance around a circle or a sphere

constellation (kahn • stel • LAY • shun) — a group of stars that seems to form a shape in the sky

degree (dih • GREE) — one of the 360 parts into which a circle is divided

eclipse (ih • KLIPS) — the hiding of the Moon, or of all or part of the Sun, by the Earth's shadow

equator (ih • KWAY • ter) — an imaginary line around the Earth, equally distant from the North and South Poles

geometry (gee • AH • mih • tree) — the study of lines, angles, and spheres and other figures

hemisphere (HEM • iss • feer) — one half of a sphere

horizon (huh • RYZ • un) — the line where the Earth or sea seems to meet the sky because the Earth's surface is curved

international (in • ter • NASH • un • il) — between nations; across the boundaries of nations

latitude (LAT • ih • tood) — the distance of a place north or south of the equator, measured in degrees

longitude (LAWN • ji • tood) — the distance of a place east or west of the prime meridian, measured in degrees

mathematician (math • ih • muh • TISH • in) — an expert in using numbers; one who studies arithmetic, geometry, algebra, etc.

meridian (mer • ID • ee • yan) — a line of longitude

navigator (NAV • ih • gay • ter) — a person who figures the course, or path, that a ship or airplane will take

parallel (PAIR • uh • lil) — lines the same distance apart and going in the same direction, as railroad tracks

planet (PLAN • it) — a large object that orbits a star; the Sun has nine planets

polar (POH • ler) — near the North Pole or the South Pole

poles (POHLZ) — the points at the top (North Pole) and bottom (South Pole) of the Earth's sphere

predict (prih • DIKT) — to tell ahead of time what will happen

radio beacon (RAY • dee • o BEE • kun) — a beam of radio waves sent out from a fixed position to guide ships or airplanes

rays (RAYZ) — energy traveling outward from an object such as the Sun

satellite (SAT • il • ite) — a body that revolves around a heavenly body; a Moon is a natural satellite, while *Sputnik I* was an artificial satellite

space probe (SPAISS PROHB) — an unmanned spacecraft sent to study heavenly bodies

time zone (TYME ZOHN) — a 15-degree-wide area of the Earth from east to west. Every place in this area has the same time.

Tropic of Cancer (TRAH • pik uv KAN • ser) — an imaginary circle around the Earth, located at 23½ degrees north of the equator

Tropic of Capricorn (TRAH • pik uv KAP • rih • korn) — an imaginary circle around the Earth, located at 23½ degrees south of the equator

universe (YOO • nih • verse) — all of space and everything in it

INDEX

About the Author

   Paul P. Sipiera is a professor of earth sciences at William Rainey
Harper College in Palatine, Illinois. His principal research interests
are in the study of meteorites and volcanic rocks. He has
participated in the United States Antarctic Research Program and
is a member of The Explorers Club. He is currently serving as
president of the Planetary Studies Foundation. When he is not
studying science, he can be found traveling the world or working
on his farm in Galena, Illinois.